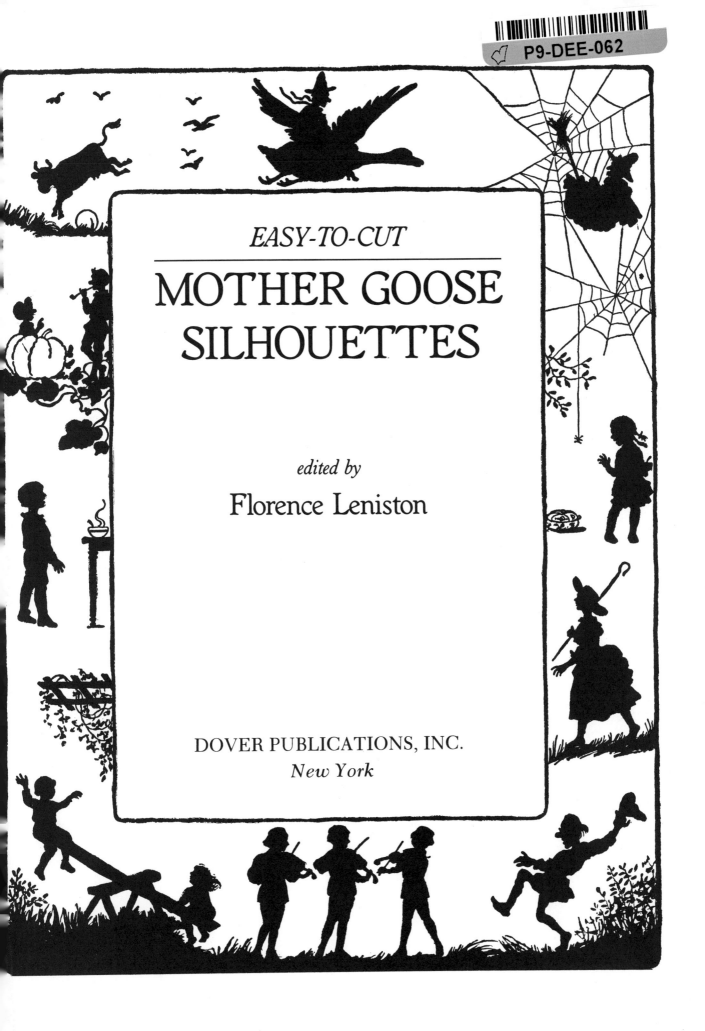

EASY-TO-CUT

MOTHER GOOSE SILHOUETTES

edited by

Florence Leniston

DOVER PUBLICATIONS, INC.
New York

Published in Canada by General Publishing Company, Ltd., 30 Lesmill Road, Don Mills, Toronto, Ontario.

Published in the United Kingdom by Constable and Company, Ltd., 3 The Lanchesters, 162–164 Fulham Palace Road, London W6 9ER.

Easy-to-Cut Mother Goose Silhouettes, first published by Dover Publications, Inc., in 1990, is a new collection of designs from *Mother Goose Silhouette Designs: 12 Artistic Drawings of Mother Goose Favorites* by Penny Ross, originally published by the Ideal School Supply Co., Chicago, 1923, and *Cut Out Pictures from Mother Goose Our Children Love,* M. A. Donohue & Co., Chicago and New York, n.d.

DOVER *Pictorial Archive* SERIES

International Standard Book Number: 0-486-26450-5

Manufactured in the United States of America
Dover Publications, Inc., 31 East 2nd Street, Mineola, N.Y. 11501

INTRODUCTION

Imagine that you are a child of days past—the early decades of this century, to be more specific. A parent, or some other attentive but frugal adult who brings you safe, inexpensive toys, comes home with two books of silhouettes for you to play with, and lends you a dainty pair of scissors—perhaps sewing scissors—of a size that fits your little hand and lets you make nimble cuts.

On the cover of one book, you see a familiar image—old Mother Goose, the legendary hostess from your favorite books of nursery rhymes, sitting in stately fashion upon a soaring gander! The cover of the other book shows a pretty child seated on the floor, completely absorbed in cutting the silhouettes out of a book just like the ones you have in front of you. These cover illustrations entice you to begin cutting out the pictures inside. When you do, you see that these books are very clever paper devices. On the front of each page is the outline of a Mother Goose character, or more than one, accompanied by objects that pertain to the same rhyme. The reverse side of the page is printed completely black. You discover that when you cut along the outline of the character on the front and then turn over the cut-out character, you have a perfect silhouette! And when you cut out the other objects in the picture, you find that they make wonderful little accessories that can be arranged around the main characters in very amusing ways.

To bring back the experience of having old-time silhouette books to play with, two books of Mother Goose silhouettes—one from the 1920s, the other thought to be from about the same time—have been preserved, complete with copies of their front covers, in this special collection. Silhouettes were indeed a popular pastime in those days, as they had been for almost two centuries previously. They kept children busy for hours and were utilized by adults too, providing inexpensive decorations for around the house.

The silhouettes herein can be used as household decorations, incorporated into artwork, or even mounted onto cardboard and played with as dolls. Many of the designs have multiple pieces. These can be arranged in any manner desired for decorative purposes, or used as accessories in play.

Quaint and soothing, the designs are ideal for decoupage, decorating furniture, trimming gift cards or album covers, or framing. They would be especially appropriate decorative additions to children's rooms, applied to the headboards of beds or the backs of little chairs, or hung on the walls.

A small pair of scissors, with a sharp, narrow point, is the only tool needed to make the silhouettes. First choose a design and remove the entire page from the book, either by cutting as closely as possible to the fold in the center or by removing the staples holding the pages of the book together. Cut carefully all the way around the outlines of each separate figure in the design. You will have to make an effort to cut smooth lines; otherwise, when the figure is turned over, the silhouette will look jagged. To make the cutting smoother, feed the paper into the scissors as you cut, holding the scissors stationary and steering the paper between the blades. An X-ACTO knife, with a #11 (or smaller) blade, is an alternative tool that would make cutting in tricky nooks and crannies much easier, and make smoother cuts, than would scissors. However, if you have never used an X-ACTO knife before, be careful; the blade is extremely sharp! Children should ask an adult to do the cutting for them, if this instrument is used.

A glue stick, applied with even strokes to the back of a silhouette, is recommended for mounting. (Liquid glue may cause the paper to wrinkle when it is applied, or it may seep beyond the edges if you try to press the silhouette flat.) Your silhouette may be glued flat or lifted from the background with dabs of silicone for extra dimension. If you mount on a background that is not white, color the cut edges with a black felt-tip pen, so that the white edges of the cut-out paper will not stand out against the background.

You do not have to cut out the designs to enjoy them. If you prefer, you can leave them uncut inside this book and just admire them as evidence that, even in the old days, clever publishers could make books into toys!

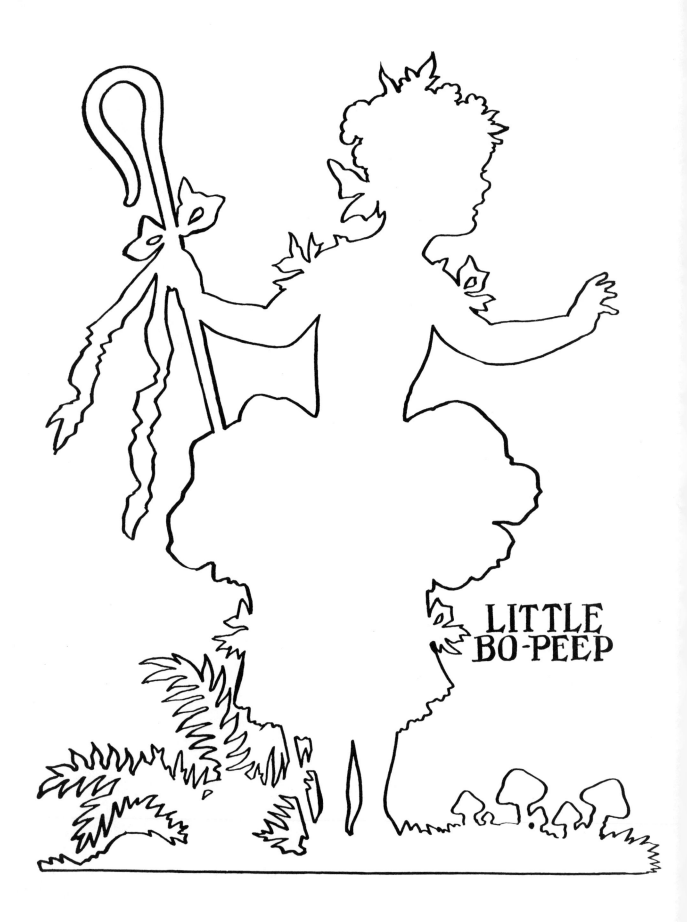

LITTLE
BO-PEEP

OLD
MOTHER
HUBBARD.

JACK BE NIMBLE

LITTLE JACK
HORNER

TOM, TOM, THE PIPER'S SON.

JACK AND JILL.

PUSSY CAT,
PUSSY CAT,
WHERE
HAVE YOU
BEEN ?

POLLY PUT
THE KETTLE
ON.

MARY HAD A
LITTLE LAMB.

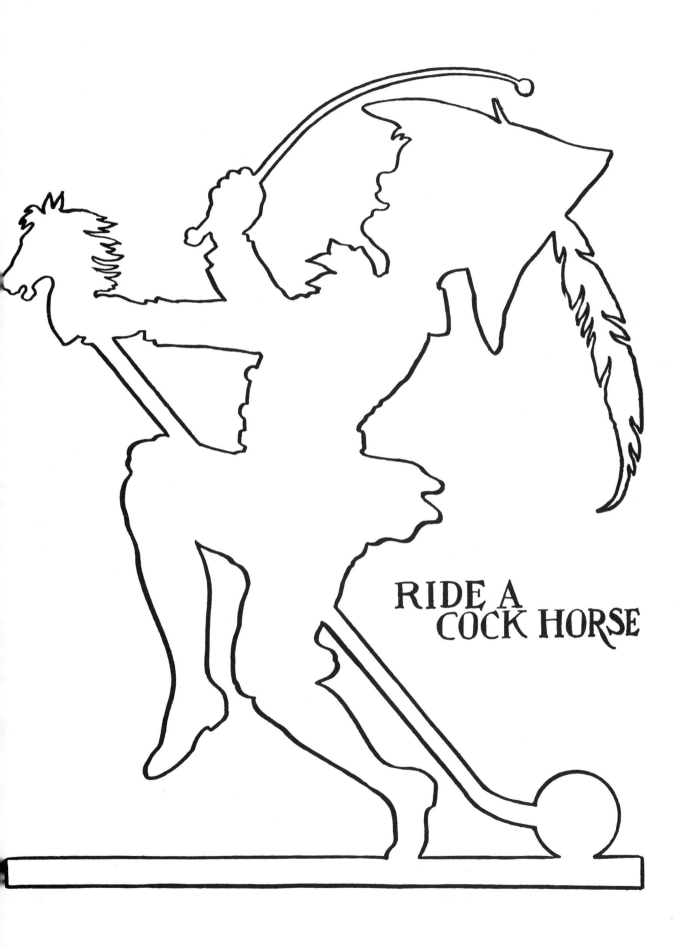

RIDE A
COCK HORSE

CUT OUT PICTURES FROM MOTHER GOOSE OUR CHILDREN LOVE

M.A. DONOHUE & CO.

CHICAGO   NEW YORK

No. 427

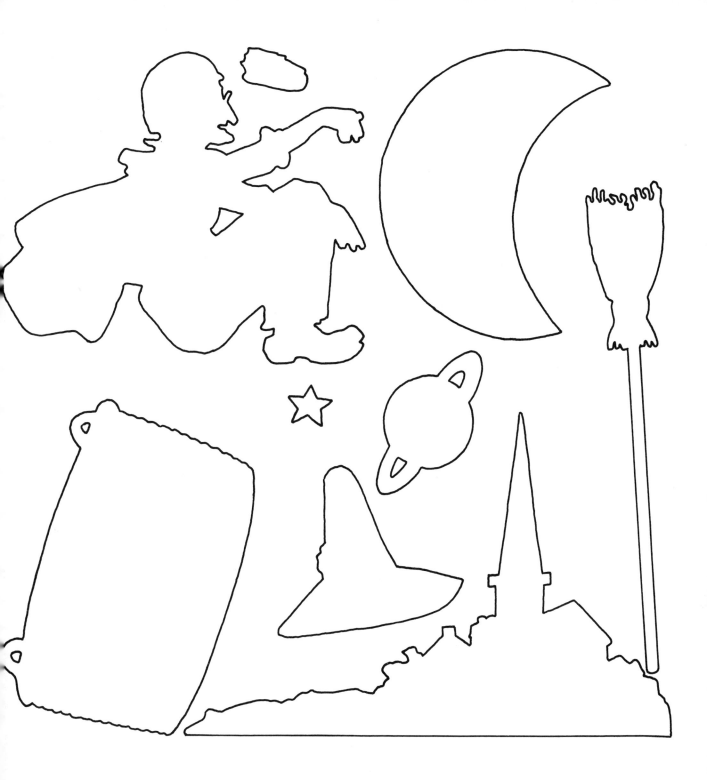

There was an old woman toss'd up in a basket,
Nineteen times as high as the moon,
Where she was going I couldn't but ask it,
For in her hand she carried a broom.

Old Mother Hubbard
Went to the cupboard,
  To get her poor dog a bone;
But when she came there
The cupboard was bare,
And so the poor dog had none.

Hey! diddle diddle,
    The cat and the fiddle,
The cow jump'd over the moon,
    The little dog laugh'd
    To see such sport,
While the dish ran after the spoon.

Peter, Peter, Pumpkin eater,
Had a wife and couldn't keep her—
He put her in a pumpkin shell,
And there he kept her very well.

See, saw, Margery Daw,
    Johnny shall have a new master:
He shall have but a penny a day,
    Because he can't work any faster.

Little Jack Horner sat in the **corner,**
    Eating a Christmas pie;
He put in his thumb and pull'd out **a**
    plum,
And said: "What a good boy am I!"

Polly, put the kettle on,
   Polly, put the kettle on,
Polly, put the kettle on,
   And let's drink tea.

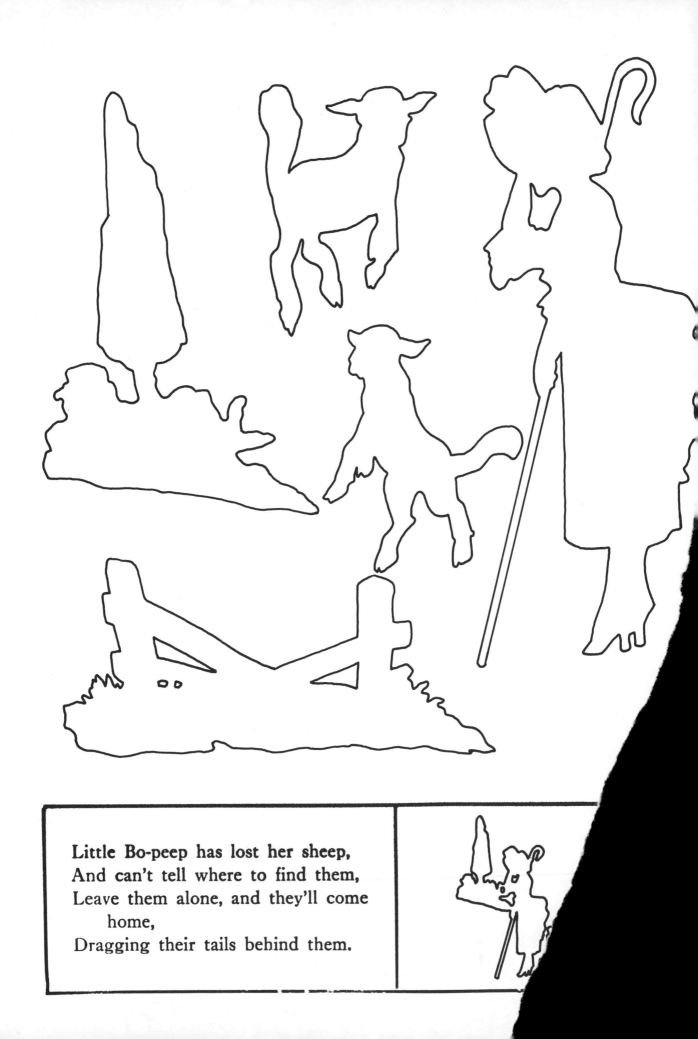

Little Bo-peep has lost her sheep,
And can't tell where to find them,
Leave them alone, and they'll come
    home,
Dragging their tails behind them.